TRIBES of NATIVE AMERICA

Ute

edited by Marla Felkins Ryan
and Linda Schmittroth

BLACKBIRCH®
PRESS

THOMSON

———*———

GALE

San Diego • Detroit • New York • San Francisco • Cleveland
New Haven, Conn. • Waterville, Maine • London • Munich

THOMSON

★

GALE

LIBRARY OF CONGRESS CATALOGING-IN-PUBLICATION DATA

Ute / Marla Felkins Ryan, book editor ; Linda Schmittroth, book editor.
   v. cm. — (Tribes of Native America)
Includes bibliographical references.
Contents: Ute name — Origins and group affiliations — History — Daily life — Customs
— Current tribal issues.
  ISBN 1-56711-723-6 (alk. paper)
  1. Ute Indians—Juvenile literature. [1. Ute Indians. 2. Indians of North America—Utah.
3. Indians of North America—Colorado. 4. Indians of North America—New Mexico.] I.
Ryan, Marla Felkins. II. Schmittroth, Linda. III. Series.

E99.U8 U84 2003
979.004'9745--dc21

2002015825

Printed in United States
10 9 8 7 6 5 4 3 2 1

Table of Contents

UTE

Name

Ute (pronounced *yoot*). The Ute call themselves *Noochew*,
which means "Ute People." The name of the state of Utah
comes from the Spanish word for the Ute—*Yutah*—which
means "high land" or "land of the sun."

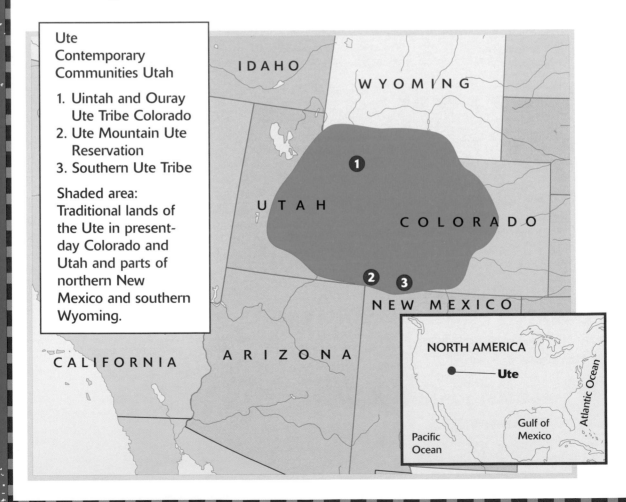

Ute
Contemporary
Communities Utah

1. Uintah and Ouray
   Ute Tribe Colorado
2. Ute Mountain Ute
   Reservation
3. Southern Ute Tribe

Shaded area:
Traditional lands of
the Ute in present-
day Colorado and
Utah and parts of
northern New
Mexico and southern
Wyoming.

IDAHO

WYOMING

UTAH

COLORADO

NEW MEXICO

CALIFORNIA

ARIZONA

NORTH AMERICA

Ute

Pacific
Ocean

Gulf of
Mexico

Atlantic
Ocean

Where are the traditional Ute lands?

Ute lands included most of Colorado and Utah and parts of New Mexico, Arizona, and Wyoming. Today, the Northern Ute live on the Uintah and Ouray Ute Reservation, with headquarters in Fort Duchesne, Utah. The Southern Ute live on a reservation in southwestern Colorado. The Ute Mountain Ute live on the Southern Ute Reservation, near Towaoc, Colorado. It includes parts of Utah and New Mexico.

Traditional dress and dance are part of Ute heritage.

What has happened to the population?

In the 1600s, there were about 4,000 Ute. In a 1990 population count by the U.S. Bureau of the Census, 7,658 people said they were Ute. These included 572 Uintah Ute, 5,626 Ute, and 1,460 Ute Mountain Ute.

The state of Utah takes its name from its native people, the Ute.

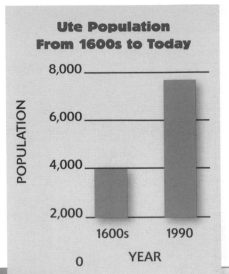

Ute Population From 1600s to Today

POPULATION	8,000
	6,000
	4,000
	2,000

1600s	1990

0   YEAR

Origins and group ties

There were seven to twelve bands, or groups, that made up the Ute. They probably left western Canada and Alaska and moved to their current homeland in the 13th century. Today, there are three main Ute groups: the Northern Ute, which is the largest; the Southern Ute; and the Ute Mountain Ute.

The Ute roamed the Great Basin and carved trails in the landscape of the West. The signs they left later helped white settlers. Though the Ute today face poverty and other problems, they have a strong spirit and sense of humor.

White settlers followed trails the Ute made in the West, including the one pictured.

HISTORY

Early relations with the Spanish

Before they met whites, the Ute lived on 79 million acres that reached from the forested slopes of the Rocky Mountains to the barren deserts of Utah. They never really formed a tribe. Instead, members were loyal to their extended family or to a small band led by a chief. They organized this way because food was scarce. Small groups had to cover a lot of land to find enough food to live.

The Ute lived in small bands led by a chief or in extended family groups.

The Ute acquired horses from the Spanish. Horses made it easy for Ute men to travel and carry out raids against other tribes.

At first, the Ute roamed their lands on foot. In the 1600s, they got horses from the Spanish. Their land was a good place to graze livestock, so they began to hunt buffalo and raise cattle and sheep. They did this rather than gather plant foods and hunt small game.

Horses made it easy for the Ute to travel far away. The Ute began to raid nearby tribes. They also attacked Spanish settlements. In these raids, the Ute took hostages, horses, and other goods. These raids made people see the Ute as a warlike group.

The Spanish, who hoped to find gold, went to Ute lands in the 1600s. One account of a Spanish meeting with the Ute noted: "They were said to be very skillful with the bow and arrow and were able to kill a buffalo with the first shot." In 1670, the Spanish signed a peace treaty with the Ute, but the Ute still did not stop their raids.

1879
Ute kill 13 U.S. soldiers and 10 Indian agency officials. This conflict becomes known as the Meeker Massacre

1895
The Weminuche band moves to the western end of the Southern Ute Reservation and becomes the Ute Mountain Ute

1896
Colorado and Utah (Northern) Ute form the Confederated Bands of Ute Indians and file claims for lands illegally taken from them

1914–1918
WWI fought in Europe

1941
Bombing at Pearl Harbor forces United States into WWII

1945
WWII ends

1950
Confederated Ute Tribes receive $31 million from the U.S. government for lands taken in the 1800s

Loss of land to Mexicans

When Mexico took over lands that would later be parts of the American Southwest in 1821, they also wanted Ute land. It was both beautiful and a good place to graze livestock. The Mexican government granted its people land in Ute territory. The Ute grew angry. As the years went by, the Ute made raids against Mexicans.

White American trappers got along well with the Ute because they did not try to steal Ute land.

When the United States won a war with Mexico in 1848, it took over Ute land. The United States agreed to respect the land grants the Mexican government had given settlers. The Ute were unhappy, but they put aside their feelings. They thought the Americans would be better trade partners than the Mexicans had been. In fact, the Ute did have good relations with American trappers and mountain men. These people did not want to take Ute land.

In 1849, the Ute and the United States signed a treaty. Ute bands said that the United States was now in charge. They promised peace and friendship. They agreed not to leave their lands without permission. They would also let U.S. citizens build military posts and Indian agencies.

Losing land in Utah and Colorado

At that time Mormons, members of the Church of Jesus Christ of Latter Day Saints, had begun to settle in Utah. Soon, they tried to convert the Ute and began to claim Ute land. Fighting resulted. This led President Abraham Lincoln to set up the Uintah Valley Reservation in 1861. In 1886, it became the Uintah and Ouray Ute Reservation.

Back in Colorado, gold was found in 1859. White miners and settlers poured in. In an 1863 treaty, some Ute agreed to give up rights to gold so they could have an 18-million-acre reservation. The bands that signed the treaty kept their own hunting grounds. The land they gave away belonged to other Ute, who were not at the treaty meetings.

Ute leaders posed with U.S. officials in Washington, D.C., after they signed the 1868 treaty that reduced Ute land in Colorado.

In 1868, most Colorado Ute signed a treaty that reduced their land to 15 million acres. Two Indian agencies, at White River and Los Pinos, were also created. Five years later, more gold was found. The Ute were forced to give up 3.4 million more acres from their Colorado reservation.

Conflict leads to massacre

Conflict continued between white settlers and Ute bands. White missionaries tried to make the Ute Christian farmers. The Ute resisted. After Colorado became a state in 1876, American settlers said that the Ute must go.

The conflict came to a head in 1879. At White River, an Indian agent named Nathan Meeker called in army troops to plow over the Ute's horseracing track. He hoped that without this amusement, they

This engraving shows Ute Indians ambushing the U.S. Army during the 1879 Meeker Massacre.

would start to farm. The Ute saw Meeker's act as a declaration of war. They warned that they would not let the army on their lands. When 150 U.S. troops came, the Ute ambushed them. In a fight that lasted almost a week, the Ute killed 13 soldiers and wounded 48 others. After two more army units got there, the troops were finally able to get to the Indian agency. They found Meeker and nine of his white workers dead. The Ute had also taken some women and children hostage.

Chief Ouray, a respected Ute leader, helped end the conflict. He won the release of the women and children. White settlers, however, saw the Meeker Massacre as one more reason to get the Ute out of Colorado. After Ouray died in 1880, the White River Ute were moved to the Uintah Reservation. Other Colorado Ute bands were sent to the Ouray Reservation, next to Uintah, in 1882.

Ute chief Ouray (center) helped free white hostages taken during the Meeker Massacre in 1879.

The allotment period

The Ute did not become farmers as fast as white Americans hoped. Many Americans also thought too much land had been set aside for Indians. In response, Congress passed the General Allotment Act in 1887.

The Ute Mountain Reservation (pictured) became the new home of the Colorado Ute in 1887.

This law was meant to speed up the process by which Indians would become more like white Americans. Reservation land was split into plots (allotments). These would be owned by individual Indians rather than by the whole tribe. The rest of the land was opened to white settlement.

The Ute did not like the allotment law. They did not want to farm. They also did not think individual people should own land. Some Ute resisted. These people lived at the western end of the Southern Ute Reservation. Their land became the Ute Mountain Ute Reservation. Land at the Southern Ute Reservation and the Uintah and Ouray Ute Reservation was given to Indians. The rest was sold. As a result, both reservations became checkerboards of Indian-owned and non-Indian-owned land.

The Ute in modern times

In 1896, the Colorado and Utah (Northern) Ute formed the Confederated Bands of Ute Indians. They asked the U.S. government to pay them back for land taken in treaties and the allotment law. In 1950, the Ute won $31.7 million. Since then, they have held many talks with local governments. They hope to clear up issues such as hunting and water rights. They have had some success. For example, they were allowed to hunt at times other than the state-ordered hunting season. They have also faced frustrating delays, though.

Ute leaders, such as Ernest House Sr. (right) and Howard Richards (second from right), continue to work with state and local governments to regain lost rights and property.

Some members of the Native American Church eat peyote to help them have visions.

Religion

The Ute believe in a Supreme Being and a number of lesser gods. There are gods of war and peace as well as floods. The Ute also have faith in life after death. They think a good spirit will lead them to the so-called Happy Hunting Ground when they die. The Ute also have evil spirits called the skinwalkers. Long ago, skinwalkers were evil Navajo warriors who could change into coyotes or foxes. The Ute believe skinwalkers can steal a person's soul.

Some Utah Ute became Mormons in the 1800s. Later, in 1898, a Catholic Church was built in Ignacio, Colorado. Some Southern Ute joined it. Many Ute today are part of the Native American Church. It was formed in Oklahoma in 1918. The church brought together several groups who had practiced the peyote (pronounced *pay-OH-tee*) religion since the 1880s. Peyote is a kind of cactus. A person who eats it may see visions.

Government

The Ute were split into large family groups or small independent bands. The bands were led by a chief, chosen for his wisdom or skills.

After they began to hunt buffalo, the Ute joined larger groups and had more powerful leaders. These leaders took charge when the camp moved. They also led hunts and war parties.

After many years under the power of the U.S. government, in the 1930s the three major Ute groups formed elected governments. The Uintah and Ouray Ute Reservation is run by a tribal business committee. The Ute Mountain Ute and the Southern Ute are ruled by tribal councils.

Ute Tribal elder Bennett Thompson served as a member of a committee that advises the Southern Ute Tribal Council.

Economy

The early Ute were hunters and gatherers. They also traded with nearby tribes. After they had horses, they traded more. They also raised cattle and raided to get what they needed. The Ute traded dried buffalo meat and hides to Pueblo people in exchange for salt and turquoise. From the Hopi, they got red ocher, a mineral. They sometimes used it to paint their faces and bodies. From the tribes on the

The Ute had difficulty supporting themselves after their traditional way of life was outlawed, and they were forced to live on reservations.

Pacific Coast they got seashells. The Ute often stole women and children in raids and sometimes traded them. For example, the Spanish gave horses to the Ute for children to be used as slaves.

As the Ute moved to reservations, the government tried to make them become farmers. Most Ute fought this. Instead, they raised livestock and continued to hunt and gather their food.

Between the 1890s and the 1930s, it was hard for the Ute to support themselves. They lived on government food handouts and raised small herds of livestock. Many worked as day laborers. The Ute also made money from land leases.

In 1950, the Confederated Ute Tribes got $31 million from the U.S. government in a lawsuit over lands taken in the 1800s. The three major Ute groups split the money. Around that time, oil and natural gas were found on the reservations. This gave the Ute another source of income. The money helped the Ute improve their reservations. For example, modern homes were built for most of the tribe. The Northern and Southern Ute also used some of the money to start businesses. Many of these, such as motels and casinos, were related to tourism.

In some ways, though, Ute life today seems grim. By 1990, half of all Ute households had a yearly income of less than $15,000. This meant the Ute were nearly three times more likely than their white neighbors to be poor.

Today, many native peoples, including the Ute, operate casinos that bring in money for their communities.

DAILY LIFE

Cradleboards allowed Ute babies to be set down or carried on someone's back.

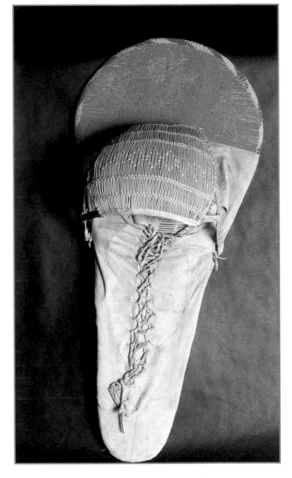

Families

The family was the basic unit of Ute society. Families were made up of parents, children, and other close relatives. Everyone helped care for children. Young girls were often the main caretakers. Girls carried babies on pieces of wood called cradleboards. Both boys and girls helped the adults gather food.

Education

For centuries, in Ute camps, everyone helped teach young children. Once they moved to reservations, Ute parents were encouraged to send their children

to government boarding schools. There, Ute children were not allowed to speak their own language. They were punished when they observed their old ways. Still, some held onto their customs.

In the 20th century, the Ute demanded public schooling for their children. Since the 1960s, Ute children have gone to public schools. Often, Ute children have trouble because they do not speak English well enough to understand their lessons. Some schools fail to respect Indian culture. Children also suffer from poverty and low self-esteem.

After the Ute moved to reservations, Ute children were encouraged to attend government-run boarding schools like this one in Colorado.

Buildings

The Ute built different kinds of homes, depending on where they lived. Most common were domed houses about 8 feet high and 15 feet around. They were made up of a pole frame covered with willow

Tepees provided easily moveable shelter for the Ute and other Indians of the Great Plains who followed the roving buffalo herds.

branches or bark. Some Ute built similar cone-shaped houses. Groups who hunted on the Great Plains had small tepees covered with elk or buffalo skin. Sweathouses were common. These were buildings for cleansing rituals. In them, water was poured over heated rocks to make steam. They are still used today.

The Ute lived in traditional homes until the 1950s. Then, new funding helped them build modern houses.

Food

Before the Ute had horses, the seven bands lived in small family groups for much of the year to gather what they could find in their lands. Food was scarce, and groups had to cover big areas to find it.

From spring until fall, family units hunted deer, elk, and antelope. They gathered seeds and wild fruits. They caught rodents and other small game. Crickets and grasshoppers were dried and mixed with berries to make fruitcake.

In late fall, the small groups rejoined the larger band. Then they left the mountains to find shelter for the winter. After they got horses in the 1600s, they went farther to hunt. Buffalo became a major source of food and clothing. The Ute loved jerky, a kind of meat that is cut into strips and dried. Jerky is still made today. Another modern dish is frybread. These plate-sized disks of bread are fried in hot fat.

Drawings on a rock in Utah show the Ute hunting elk on horseback.

Clothing

Ute women tanned hides with great skill. They used the hides of buffalo, deer, and other animals for clothing. Ute women wore long, belted dresses with leggings and moccasins. Men wore shirts, leggings, and moccasins every day. They added feathered headdresses on special occasions.

Many men painted their bodies and faces. The colors yellow and black were used in times of war. Women sometimes painted their faces and the part in their hair. Some Ute pierced their noses and put small animal bones in the hole. Others tattooed their faces with cactus thorns dipped in ashes. Both sexes wore necklaces of animal bones and juniper seeds.

Ute men wore shirts that were sometimes decorated with beads and fringe.

Ute no longer have their own shamans, so Ute who prefer traditional healing methods might seek out a Navajo medicine man like this one.

Healing practices

Among the Ute, shamans (pronounced *SHAH-munz* or *SHAY-munz*) were both healers and religious leaders. They got supernatural powers from the spirits of animals and dead people. Most shamans knelt next to a sick person and sang special curing songs. Some shamans also carried small bags that held special items, such as small drums and rattles. The objects helped the shaman heal people.

Today, there are no more old-time Ute healers. Most Ute use modern health-care facilities in urban areas. Those who prefer traditional healers may see Navajo medicine men in Arizona.

Ute had many
uses for baskets.

Arts

Ute crafts had
almost been
forgotten by the
1930s. Today, they
have been revived.
Some Ute weave
baskets and make
pottery. Others
work with beads
and leather. They
often sell these
works of art in
gift shops.

Ute artists create
beaded buckskin
bags to sell to
tourists.

Literature

Many Ute tales explained features of the natural landscape. For example, legends tell about Sleeping Ute Mountain, which looks like a sleeping Indian with a headdress. The Indian was once a Great Warrior God who was wounded and fell into a deep sleep. Blood from his wound became water. Rain clouds fell from his pockets. The blanket that covers him changes color with the seasons.

Ute tales explained the appearance of natural features such as Ute Mountain (background).

CUSTOMS

Hunting rituals

A Ute boy was viewed as a man once he proved he could bring in meat. He was not allowed to eat his first kill.

Ute disguised themselves in deerskins when they hunted deer. They wore snowshoes to hunt elk and drove the animals into deep snow before killing them.

The Sun Dance

The two most important Ute ceremonies were the Sun Dance and the Bear Dance. Both are still done each year.

This painting depicts a traditional Sun Dance.

The Sun Dance is a quest by a dancer to get power from the Great Spirit. Each dancer also represents his or her family and community. This makes the dance a way to share culture. The Sun Dance comes from a legend. In it, a man and a woman left the tribe in a time of terrible hunger. On their trip, they met a god who taught them the Sun Dance. After they came back and did the dance with the tribe, a herd of buffalo appeared. The hunger ended.

The Sun Dance ceremony includes several days of secret rituals. This is followed by a public dance done around a special pole, seen as a link to the Creator. Rituals involve fasts and prayers. The Ute also smoke as part of the ceremony.

The Bear Dance

The Bear Dance takes place every spring. It honors the grizzly bear, which gave the Ute wisdom and taught them to survive. In the early days, the Bear Dance was held at the time when bears came out of hibernation. The dance was meant to wake up the bear so it could help the people find nuts and berries.

The Bear Dance lasted for four days and nights. A large, circle-shaped enclosure was built of sticks. This represented a bear's den. Music was played inside the enclosure to act as the thunder that wakes up the sleeping bears.

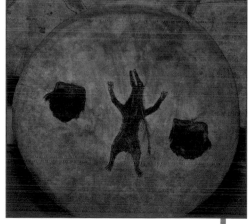

Drums like this one were used during the yearly Bear Dance.

Current tribal issues

One of the issues the Ute deal with today is water rights. The Ute Mountain Ute in Colorado had no safe drinking water on the reservations until the mid-1990s, when part of a $73 million water project was completed. The rest of the project has not yet been funded.

Ute chief Ouray worked tirelessly for the rights of his people.

Notable people

Chief Ouray (c.1833–1880) was a spokesman for the Ute. Born in Taos, New Mexico, he was a shepherd on Mexican ranches during his youth. He moved to Colorado at the age of 18 and became a leader. In 1867, Ouray helped put down a Ute revolt. In 1868, he went to Washington, D.C., as a spokesman for the Ute bands. His work helped the Ute keep 16 million acres of land. In 1872, Ouray again visited Washington. The Ute were pressured to give up 4 million acres in return for a yearly payment of $25,000. In 1880, Ouray went to Washington once more. There, he signed the treaty that moved the White River Ute to the Uintah and Ouray Ute Reservation. Ouray died in 1880. Without his strong voice for their interests, the Ute were moved from Colorado the next year.

Another notable Ute is tribal leader Walkara (1801–1855). He was perhaps the most powerful American Indian leader in the Great Basin area from 1830 until his death.

For More Information

Carrier, Jim. *West of the Divide: Voices from a Ranch and a Reservation.* Golden, Colorado: Fulcrum, 1992.

Dutton, Bertha P. *The Rancheria, Ute, and Southern Paiute Peoples.* Englewood Cliffs, NJ: Prentice-Hall, 1975.

—. "The Ute Indians." *American Indians of the Southwest.* Albuquerque: University of New Mexico Press, 1983.

Pettit, Jan. *Utes: The Mountain People.* Colorado Springs, CO: Century One Press, 1982.

Southern Ute Homepage
http://www.southern-ute.nsn.us/index.html

Uintah and Ouray Reservation Homepage
http://www.uwin.com/ute/

Ute Mountain Ute Homepage
http://www.aclin.org/other/society_culture/native_american/ute/index.html

This stone monument in Colorado was built in memory of Chief Ouray and his wife.

Glossary

Bands groups

Raid an attack on land or a settlement, usually to steal food and other goods

Reservation land set aside and given to Native Americans

Ritual something that is custom or done in a certain way

Tribe a group of people who live together in a community

Index